American
Politics Today

The Presidential Election Process

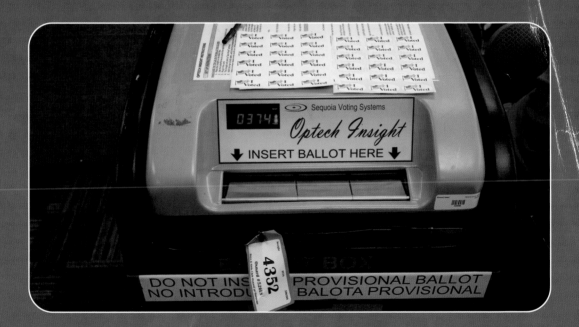

Holly Lynn Anderson

ELDORADO INK

Eldorado Ink
PO Box 100097
Pittsburgh, PA 15233
www.eldoradoink.com

Produced by OTTN Publishing, Stockton, New Jersey

CPSIA compliance information: Batch#MAP2016.
For further information, contact Eldorado Ink at info@eldoradoink.com.

First printing

1 3 5 7 9 8 6 4 2

Library of Congress Cataloging-in-Publication Data

Names: Anderson, Holly Lynn, author.
Title: The presidential election process / Holly Lynn Anderson.
Description: Pittsburgh, PA : Eldorado Ink, 2016. | Series: American politics
  today | Includes bibliographical references and index.
Identifiers: LCCN 2015048944| ISBN 9781619000940 (hc) | ISBN 9781619001022
  (pb) | ISBN 9781619001107 (trade)
Subjects: LCSH: Presidents—United States—Election—Juvenile literature.
Classification: LCC JK524 .A758 2016 | DDC 324.60973—dc23
LC record available at http://lccn.loc.gov/2015048944

For information about custom editions, special sales, or premiums,
please contact our special sales department at info@eldoradoink.com.

Table of Contents

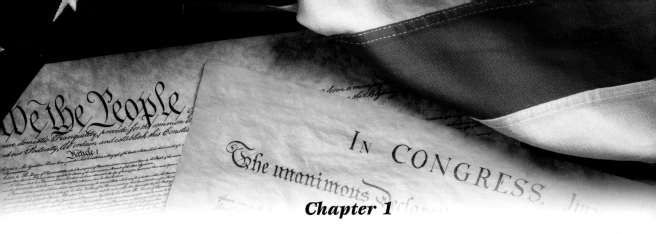

Chapter 1

An Overview of the Election Process

The basic framework for the process to elect the president of the United States was established by the founding fathers in the U.S. Constitution in 1787. This framework ensures that the highest office in the nation is held by an individual who has been chosen by the people through an orderly and peaceful election process. Participating in this orderly and peaceful transfer of power is a right and responsibility of all American citizens.

The framework for this process is specified in the Constitution, but the procedure has been modified at various times over the past 200 years. These changes have not always been without controversy. Even now, there are many different ideas about how the presidential election should be managed. People have differences of opinions as to whether the process is fair and whether all American citizens truly have an opportunity to make their voices heard.

A voter inserts a completed ballot into a voting machine in California. Citizens of the United States who are at least eighteen years of age are eligible to vote, so long as they register with their state voting agency and conform to certain other rules.

One problem today is that many Americans don't take their responsibility to vote for their leaders seriously. On average, in the last few presidential elections only about 58 percent of eligible voters actually cast ballots. Some experts believe that low voter turnout is due to an inherent distrust of the system. This distrust, in turn, may be partly based on a failure to understand the complicated process of American presidential elections. Many citizens believe they can't make a difference. But every vote does count and the 2000 presidential election—in which only 54 percent of eligible voters participated—made that clear.

THE CONTROVERSIAL PRESIDENTIAL ELECTION OF 2000

In 2000 the United States experienced possibly the most controversial presidential election in history. A total of 50,999,899 people voted for the Democratic Party candidate, Al Gore. A total of 50,456,002 people voted for the Republican Party candidate, George W. Bush. As these numbers show, over half a million more Americans wanted Gore as their president than those who wanted Bush. However, on January 20, 2001, George W. Bush was inaugurated as the forty-third president of the United States.

How could this happen? How could the voting majority choose one candidate but another person become president? The answer is that the votes of the citizens (the popular votes) are not directly responsible for electing the president. The popular votes are used to determine the winning candidate in each state. The president is formally chosen by the Electoral College, a group of electors picked by the winning political party in each state. Members of the Electoral College vote to determine which candidate becomes president. In 2000, George W. Bush won the popular vote in thirty states and received 271 electoral votes. Al Gore won the popular vote in twenty states and received 266 electoral votes. So, George W. Bush was declared the winner.

This was not the only election in U.S. history in which the winner of the popular vote did not become president. This had previously occurred in 1824, 1876, and 1888. But it was the only time in over one hundred years that the popular vote and the electoral vote didn't

2000 Presidential Election

George W. Bush (Republican)
50,456,002 popular votes (47.9%)
271 electoral votes

Al Gore (Democratic)
50,999,987 popular votes (48.4%)
266 electoral votes

Ralph Nader (Green)
2,882,955 popular votes (2.7%)

Patrick Buchanan (Reform)
448,895 popular votes (0.4%)

*One of the three electors from the District of Columbia, pledged to the Democratic Party, submitted a blank ballot to protest the outcome of the election.

match. None of the voters in 2000 were alive the previous three times it occurred, so it seemed like something new and unusual. Many people were surprised that it could happen and concerned, as well as confused, thinking that the wishes of the voters had not been honored. But the system worked exactly the way it was supposed to work, according to the framework established by the Constitution. The secret to making every vote count and ensuring that every voter's wishes are honored is to fully understand and participate in the election system.

MAKING A DIFFERENCE

Electing the president of the United States is complicated. There are many steps in the process, beginning long before the voters actually make their selection. Candidates must first meet the eligibility requirements, then they must officially declare their candidacy. The political parties hold caucuses and primaries to determine the leading candidates, and then national conventions where the party's presidential candidate is praised and celebrated. The candidates travel the country speaking to voters, and participate in nationally televised debates. Along the way, each party's campaign staff develops strategies that will give their candidate an advantage, spending millions of dollars on advertising.

Every citizen has the right to participate in the process to choose the country's top leader. Everyone needs to understand the process and how to participate fully in that process. It is also crucial to understand the ways the process continues to evolve. Every citizen has a right to take part in the decisions made to change and improve the process. The opportunities to participate are there, but you have to know where to find them.

Chapter 2

Eligibility Requirements

A rticle II, Section 1 of the Constitution sets the eligibility requirements for the presidency and the length of time the president can serve. These requirements have been in place since the Constitution was first written in 1787. There are only three rules determining who is eligible to become president of the United States: (1) Candidates must be natural-born citizens, (2) candidates must be at least thirty-five years old, and (3) candidates must have lived in the United States for at least fourteen years.

In 1804, the Twelfth Amendment to the Constitution clarified the eligibility requirements for vice president. The amendment stated that any person who was ineligible to be president was also ineligible to be vice president. This had not been specifically stated in the original wording of the Constitution. Since the vice president could, at any time, be required to assume the office of president, it was determined that the eligibility requirements should be the same for both.

If the president is not able to continue serving due to illness, death, resignation, or removal from office, the vice president is elevated to the office of president. This has occurred nine times in American history. The Twenty-Fifth Amendment, ratified in 1967, clarified the procedure by which the vice president becomes president.

The Twenty-Second Amendment to the U.S. Constitution, ratified in 1951, limits the number of times that a person can be elected president. The most a person can serve is two four-year terms. Before this amendment was adopted, a president could serve an unlimited number of terms, although only one president, Franklin D. Roosevelt, was ever elected to more than two four-year terms. There remains nothing in the Constitution that prevents someone from serving as vice president for more than two terms.

NATURAL BORN CITIZEN

Over the years, there has been discussion about exactly what the Constitution means by "natural born citizen." The typical interpretation of this phrase is a person who was born in the United States to parents who are American citizens. But what about those born in U.S. territories or overseas military bases? What about children of foreign diplomats who were born in the United States? What about children born to parents who are U.S. citizens that live in the United States, but are traveling outside the United States when the child is born? What about children born to parents who are citizens of other countries who happen to be traveling in the United States when the child is born? Over time, these questions have been resolved by additional amendments and rulings by federal judges.

Shortly after the Constitution went into effect, the Naturalization Act of 1790 clarified that children of U.S. citizens born outside the United States would be considered "natural born citizens." The text of this law specifically uses the term *natural born citizen*, just as in the presidential eligibility wording. So it is clear that these children are eligible for the presidency.

In 1868, prompted by the freeing of slaves at the end of the Civil War, the Fourteenth Amendment to the Constitution granted citizenship to all persons born in the United States, as well as those who have been naturalized. Naturalization is a process in which foreign-born citizens of other countries may become U.S. citizens by living a minimum number of years in the country and completing a legal application process and citizenship test.

During his 2008 presidential campaign, questions were raised about whether John McCain, the Republican Party's candidate, qualified as a "natural born citizen." McCain was born on August 29, 1936, in the Panama Canal Zone, which at the time was a U.S. territory. His parents were both U.S. citizens. McCain's father, an officer in the U.S. Navy, was stationed in the Canal Zone. Many legal scholars agreed that McCain met the criteria to serve as president—but had he won the election, his eligibility might have been challenged.

The Courts have ruled that naturalized citizens are not the same as natural born citizens. A naturalized citizen possesses most of the same rights as natural-born citizens, including the right to vote. However, naturalized citizens do not meet the Constitutional requirements to serve as president.

The issue of natural born versus naturalized citizens was further clarified in the late nineteenth century. A man named Wong Kim Ark had been born in 1871 in San Francisco to parents who were natives of China, but who were living and working in the United States. As a young adult, Wong Kim Ark traveled outside the United States; when he returned, he was not allowed to enter the U.S. due to laws that had been passed restricting Chinese immigration. He challenged this in a case that eventually reached the U.S. Supreme Court. In *United States v. Wong Kim Ark* (1898), the Supreme Court ruled that Wong Kim Ark was a natural born U.S. citizen. This was an important decision, as it meant that any child born in the United States was a "natural born citizen," even if their parents are not citizens.

There is a distinction, however, as children born in the United States to foreign diplomats represent a separate case. Diplomats are considered "attached" to foreign embassies, which are not considered land under the control of the United States. Therefore, federal courts

CERTIFICATE OF LIVE BIRTH

STATE OF HAWAII   **CERTIFICATE OF LIVE BIRTH**   DEPARTMENT OF HEALTH

FILE NUMBER **151**   **61 10641**

1a. Child's First Name (Type or print)	1b. Middle Name	1c. Last Name
BARACK	HUSSEIN	OBAMA, II

2. Sex	3. This Birth	4. If Twin or Triplet, Was Child Born	5a. Birth Date	Month	Day	Year	5b. Hour
Male	Single ☑ Twin ☐ Triplet ☐	1st ☐ 2nd ☐ 3rd ☐		August	4,	1961	7:24 P.M.

6a. Place of Birth: City, Town or Rural Location	6b. Island
Honolulu	Oahu

6c. Name of Hospital or Institution (If not in hospital or institution, give street address)	6d. Is Place of Birth Inside City or Town Limits? If no, give judicial district
Kapiolani Maternity & Gynecological Hospital	Yes ☑ No ☐

7a. Usual Residence of Mother: City, Town or Rural Location	7b. Island	7c. County and State or Foreign Country
Honolulu	Oahu	Honolulu, Hawaii

7d. Street Address	7e. Is Residence Inside City or Town Limits? If no, give judicial district
6085 Kalanianaole Highway	Yes ☑ No ☐

7f. Mother's Mailing Address	7g. Is Residence on a Farm or Plantation?
	Yes ☐ No ☑

8. Full Name of Father			9. Race of Father
BARACK	HUSSEIN	OBAMA	African

10. Age of Father	11. Birthplace (Island, State or Foreign Country)	12a. Usual Occupation	12b. Kind of Business or Industry
25	Kenya, East Africa	Student	University

13. Full Maiden Name of Mother			14. Race of Mother
STANLEY	ANN	DUNHAM	Caucasian

15. Age of Mother	16. Birthplace (Island, State or Foreign Country)	17a. Type of Occupation Outside Home During Pregnancy	17b. Date Last Worked
18	Wichita, Kansas	None	

I certify that the above stated information is true and correct to the best of my knowledge.	18a. Signature of Parent or Other Informant	Parent ☑ Other ☑	18b. Date of Signature
	(Stanley) Ann Dunham Obama		8-7-61

I hereby certify that this child was born alive on the date and hour stated above.	19a. Signature of Attendant	M.D. ☑ D.O. ☐ Midwife ☐ Other ☐	19b. Date of Signature
	David A. Sinclair		8-8-61

20. Date Accepted by Local Reg.	21. Signature of Local Registrar	22. Date Accepted by Reg. General
AUG -8 1961	*U.K. Lee*	AUG -8 1961

23. Evidence for Delayed Filing or Alteration

During the 2008 election, conspiracy theories began to circulate that Barack Obama had actually been born in Kenya, not Hawaii, as he claimed. The rumors persisted even after he was elected. In 2011, to quell the rumors, the White House released a copy of Obama's birth certificate, showing that he had in fact been born in Hawaii on August 4, 1961, which had become a U.S. state in 1959—two years prior to his birth.

have ruled that children born in the United States to foreign diplomats are not considered natural-born citizens.

Subsequent court decisions have determined that natural born citizenship is granted by the Constitution to any person born in the United States or in any location under its legal jurisdiction, such as U.S. territories and military bases located in foreign countries. Such persons are considered natural born citizens even if their parents were not U.S. citizens. Children born to U.S citizens while they are traveling outside the jurisdiction of the United States are also considered to be "natural born."

CHECKING AND CERTIFYING ELIGIBILITY

Despite the attention given to the eligibility requirements for serving as president, there is no national process by which candidates are certified as eligible. No one at the federal level reviews a candidate's eligibility prior to an election, or even after an election. People may announce their candidacy, begin raising funds, and participate in the debates without ever proving their eligibility. The best opportunity to certify eligibility for candidates is at the state level, when candidates are approved to be added to the voting ballot.

Each state determines which candidates are placed on the voting ballots in that state. The chief election officer is usually the state's attorney general. That officer is responsible for making decisions about adding candidates to the ballot. The requirements are slightly different in each state, but usually candidates must officially declare their candidacy, pay a filing fee, and submit a petition with voter signatures, proving that the citizens in that state want them on the ballot. Different states require a different number of signatures, ranging from 500 to 2,000 for candidates of the two major parties; third-party candidates may need to collect tens of thousands of signatures to be included on a state's ballot. State officials generally check the candidates if there is a question about whether they meet the minimum age requirement, but they rarely determine eligibility in terms of the "natural born citizen" requirement.

Some political analysts have suggested that the chief election officer in each state should make a formal eligibility certification, including natural born citizen status, for each candidate, before allowing the prospective candidate's name to be placed on the ballot. This would eliminate accusations between candidates and from the press regarding eligibility. Other analysts believe the eligibility certification should be made when candidates are invited to participate in the debates. However, the debate managers do not have any authority over the state ballots and without a certification by state officials, ineligible candidates could still end up on voting ballots.

Recently, eligibility questions were raised against John McCain in his bid for president in 2008, against Barack Obama in 2008 and 2012, and against Ted Cruz in the early stages of the 2016 election campaign. Currently, as many as eleven states have proposed legislation requiring eligibility certifications, including requiring candidates to submit birth certificates to state election officials. However, many of the laws have faced extensive debate and some have been withdrawn before coming to a vote or held back in committee. Eligibility questions will no doubt continue to cause controversy until a formal certification process is implemented.

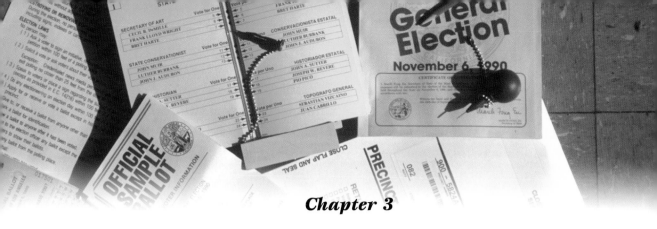

Chapter 3

Primaries and Caucuses

A fter a candidate declares his or her intention to run for president, the next step is to gain the support of his or her political party. To win the party's nomination, the candidate must receive more votes in the primaries and caucuses than other candidates.

Rules for the nomination process are not spelled out in the Constitution. No political parties existed when the Constitution was written in 1787. As political parties developed, so did the need for a process to nominate presidential candidates. The idea of primaries and caucuses emerged as a way for each political party to determine the candidate that would represent them in the election.

The rules for holding primaries and caucuses are determined by each state's party committees. Each party decides on a state-by-state basis whether to hold either a primary or a caucus. The primaries and caucuses are held separately for Democrats and Republicans, the two major political parties.

PARTY CAUCUSES

A *caucus* is simply a meeting of political party members. In a caucus, the registered party members discuss the people from that party who have announced their candidacy. There could be as few as three or four candidates or as many as ten or more. There is no set number. It all depends on how many people decide to run for office.

Registered party members participating in the caucus are called delegates. Individual delegates will have a favorite candidate and will attempt to convince other delegates to vote for that person. After the discussion, the members vote by raising their hands as each candidate's name is called. It is not a secret ballot.

State caucuses are held in a series. Precinct-level caucuses are held first, followed by caucuses at the county level, the district level, and then the state level. Results from all the precinct caucuses are added together at the county level. Then county-level results are added together and taken to the district level. Finally, all district results are added together and taken to the state level.

Precinct-level caucuses receive the most media attention because they are an early indication of which candidate is most popular with party members. But the entire process, from precinct to state, usually takes five or six months, between January and June, prior to the general election in November. During the caucuses, party members not only vote for their favorite candidates but also for party members nominated to attend the party's national convention.

Members elected during the state caucuses attend the party's national convention as representatives of the state party. These are the convention delegates. The delegates vote during the convention to officially nominate the one candidate who will represent that party in the general election. Some caucuses are "winner take all," which means that all the delegates for that state are pledged to the candidate receiving the most overall votes. But some states have "proportional" caucuses, meaning the delegates are assigned to vote at the convention for all candidates receiving votes in the state caucus, based on the proportion of votes each one received in the state caucus. For example, if Susan Miller receives 50 percent of the state-level caucus votes, 50 percent of the delegates to the convention will be pledged to Susan Miller. If Adrian Rodriguez receives 25 percent of the caucus votes, 25 percent of the delegates will be pledged to Adrian Rodriguez. And if John Zambelli receives 25 percent of the caucus votes, the remaining

25 percent of the delegates will be pledged to vote for John Zambelli at the convention. Whether a state has a winner-take-all or a proportional caucus depends on the party's rules. These rules are not permanent and can change for each election.

The caucus was the original method used by all states to determine party candidates and was developed as political parties first took shape. Today only a few states still determine party candidates by caucus votes. Starting in the early 1900s, many states began to switch to primaries, believing a direct vote by party members using a secret ballot would be fairer, and now the majority of states use the primary method.

PRIMARIES

In a primary election, voters participate in a secret ballot, just as in the general election. There are several different types of primaries and each state party committee decides which kind it will hold. In a closed primary, only registered party members may vote in that party's primary. Voters must show proof of party registration to vote in a closed primary. In other words, in a closed primary, registered Democrats may only choose from among the Democratic candidates and registered Republicans may only choose from among the Republican candidates. (In addition to selecting a candidate, voters also select the delegates to the party convention during the primaries.) Independent voters—that is, those not registered with one of the two major parties—are not allowed to vote in closed primaries.

In an open primary, voters may participate in either the Democratic primary or the Republican primary. A voter is not required to declare a party affiliation and may decide to vote in either primary. That means that Republicans could vote for a Democratic candidate, and vice versa. Independent voters are also allowed to vote in either party's primary. In open primaries, members of one party may decide to vote in the other party's primary in an attempt to skew the results, hoping that the party will select a weaker candidate that will be easier for their candidate to run against in the general election.

There are also a couple of variations on the closed and open primaries. In a semi-closed primary, both registered party members and independents may participate. But registered party members may only vote for those running in their declared party. In a semi-open primary, all registered voters may participate, but they must request a specific party ballot when they check in at the voting location. This ballot will show only those candidates running for that party's nomination. So, voters must still choose from among the candidates running under a particular party banner.

A state's political party's decision to hold a caucus or a primary (and what type of primary) is not a permanent decision. Before each election, the party decides which type of event to hold. This decision is usually made the year before the election year. Voters need to stay informed about the parties' decisions. This can be done by contacting each party directly, by visiting the party's website, or by visiting other political websites monitoring the election. Not only is it crucial to know whether the party will hold a caucus or a primary, but it is also important to know when the events will be held.

SCHEDULING STATE CAUCUSES AND PRIMARIES

New Hampshire has a state law that requires its primary to be the first in the nation, and the governor is expected to do whatever is necessary to see that it is, including moving the date of the primary if any other state attempts to be first. Iowa holds the first caucus. The New Hampshire Primary and the Iowa Caucus are typically held in January or February of the election year. These two events always receive a lot of attention from the candidates and the media. Candidates typically schedule many personal appearances and also spend a lot of money on advertising in New Hampshire and Iowa. Being first in the nation is very beneficial both politically and financially to these two states.

Over time, primaries and caucuses have become "front-loaded," or scheduled by more and more states toward the beginning of the year. States are opting to hold primaries and caucuses earlier and earlier to have a perceived greater impact on the final decisions and to lure candidates to the state for public appearances. Most states now schedule primaries and caucuses in February and March. "Super Tuesdays" are

Donald Trump, a candidate for the Republican Party's presidential nomination in 2016, speaks to New Hampshire voters at an event in Manchester. Because New Hampshire holds the first primary of each presidential election cycle, candidates spend an extraordinary amount of time and money wooing voters of the small state.

Tuesdays in February or March when as many as fifteen states hold primaries and caucuses on the same date. Many other votes follow during the next couple of weeks. All presidential primaries and caucuses are completed by the end of June.

It is very important for candidates to be successful early in the process. When a candidate wins a primary or a caucus, he or she gains momentum and attracts more media attention and financial donations. If a candidate does not do well in the early months, he or she is usually forced to drop out of the race. Front-loading requires candidates to begin campaigning early, typically in the summer of the year before the election year. Some analysts say that front-loading has created an extremely long campaign season, which bores the voters, causing them to lose interest. Another problem with front-loading by states is that it forces candidates to choose which states they will visit for public appearances. With so many events in the first three months of the year, all candidates cannot make it to all states in advance of the vote. Some voters are not able to see the candidates in person. Also, as candidates drop out of the race, voters in states with later primaries or caucuses may have fewer candidates to choose from on the ballot.

PROPOSED SCHEDULING CHANGES

Several proposals have been introduced over the years for changes to the nomination process. Most recommend completely removing caucuses from the process and changing the primary schedule to avoid the front-loading issues. In many cases, analysts have suggested holding only open primaries. However, the major political parties are reluctant to support any proposal that might increase the influence of independent voters and either lessen the power of the parties in general or minimize party control over the selection of the nominees specifically.

One proposal calls for a national primary, in which all states hold the nomination election on the same day. Supporters of this proposal claim it will solve the front-loading issue and do away with states competing to see which elections can be the earliest. Opponents of this proposal claim the national primary day will only make things worse, especially for candidates with less money. They believe some candidates would have an even harder time raising enough money for public appearances and advertising if the primaries were not conducted over a several-month period. The leaders of the two major political parties have generally opposed a national primary day, believing they would have less influence over the selection of the nominees, especially if it were set up as an open primary with equal access by independent voters.

Another proposal, called the Delaware Plan, recommends grouping states into "pods," based on population. The primaries would then be held in four groups: (1) the thirteen smallest states, (2) the next thirteen smallest states, (3) the next twelve medium-sized states, and (4) the twelve largest states. The primaries would be held separately, in that order. Those in favor of this plan believe it would provide an incentive for candidates to arrange for more personal appearances in

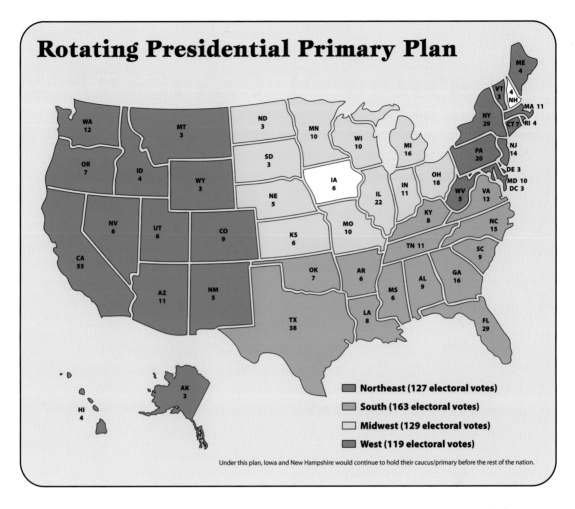

Rotating Presidential Primary Plan

Northeast (127 electoral votes)
South (163 electoral votes)
Midwest (129 electoral votes)
West (119 electoral votes)

Under this plan, Iowa and New Hampshire would continue to hold their caucus/primary before the rest of the nation.

smaller states. Opponents of the plan believe it would favor candidates with more money. Because the pods are not based on location and states in each pod are spread out across the country, candidates with less funding might not be able to do all the traveling necessary to visit all states in each pod before the assigned primary dates and might not be able to afford advertising in all the states.

A third proposal is the Rotating Presidential Primary Plan. Under this plan, the country would be divided into four geographical regions: Northeast, South, Midwest, and West. Each group holds a comparable number of electoral votes. The order of the primaries would rotate in each election. The chart at the top of this page shows each regional group and the number of its electoral votes.

Proponents of this plan believe it solves the problem of high travel costs for the candidates, enabling them to avoid traveling back and forth across the country and keeping them in certain geographic regions for a month at a time. It would also enable the candidates to become more familiar with the key issues in particular geographic regions. Opponents believe it might encourage candidates to "camp out" in certain states with higher numbers of electoral votes for longer periods. Candidates would also know the rotation many years in advance. Some analysts think that might affect when candidates decide to run, possibly deciding to run in an election year when a region favorable to their campaign votes first.

Another suggested change to the nomination process is to keep the idea of geographic regions but use a lottery system to determine the order of the primaries, instead of having the order rotate in a predictable pattern. That way, candidates would not know in advance which region would vote first. A nonpartisan lottery commission would manage the system. The drawing would occur six months before the beginning of the primaries. Some analysts say this would solve the current problem of front-loading, but maintain the large regions, which could still be a problem for candidates with less funding.

Currently, the planning of the nomination process remains under the control of the two major parties, and they have been reluctant to make substantial changes in the process. The Republican Party recently announced a plan to move the date of their party's convention to earlier in the year, in hopes of shortening the primary season. The party would punish any state that attempted to move its primary up earlier than February by banning that state's delegation from the convention. Some proposals have been advanced in Congress to force changes in the nomination system. So far, those proposals have not received much support.

Chapter 4

Raising Money and Getting Attention

Candidates must be fund-raisers as well as policymakers. To seriously compete for a party's nomination, a candidate must raise huge sums of money—as much as $50 million. That money is spent on travel, office space and equipment, salaries for campaign staff and advisers, radio and television advertising, opinion polls, and mass mailings, plus promotional materials such as lawn signs, bumper stickers, buttons, and caps. With all the expenses involved in a campaign, it is easy to see why poorly funded candidates are at a disadvantage. It is especially important to be able to raise funds early. Having funds available in the early primaries and caucuses usually helps a candidate gain greater name recognition through early advertising and public appearances. And if a candidate has money early on in the nomination process, that often translates into a good showing in the early votes and helps ensure that more money will be available later. Contributors like to back a winner.

Before the nomination, candidates may receive funds from the federal government to assist in campaigning. To qualify for federal funding, the candidate must be able to raise $5,000 in individual contributions of $250 or less in twenty states ($100,000 total). The public funds also come with some conditions. The candidates must agree to limit the amount they spend of their own personal money to $50,000. They must also comply with the specific spending limits set for each election period. These limits apply until the party's official candidate is nominated at the convention. Some candidates, especially those with large personal fortunes, elect not to accept public money so they don't have to comply with the spending limits.

Individual citizens may give up to $2,700 to a candidate during the primary election race. Another source of funds for candidates is money from political action committees (PACs). These are committees established by corporations, labor unions, or special-interest groups specifically for fund-raising purposes. A PAC may donate up to $5,000 to a candidate during the primary election period.

The Internet now figures prominently in campaign fund-raising. Websites have few direct expenses and can reach millions of people virtually instantaneously. This has been especially helpful to candidates early in the primary race. With donation limits placed on individuals, candidates cannot rely on huge contributions from just a few

The total amount of federal election funding in past election cycles has ranged from about $73 million in 1976 to nearly $240 million in 2000. In recent elections, the total has declined tremendously. In the 2012 election cycle, the federal government provided $37.9 million in public financing. That was a decline of more than $100 million from the 2008 election cycle's total of $139.5 million. The 2012 presidential election marked the first time that both the Republican and Democratic Party nominees opted out of the public financing program for both the primary and general elections.

In 1992, a wealthy Texas businessman named Ross Perot ran an independent campaign to become president. During the campaign Perot spent $65 million of his own money, mostly on television advertising. On election day Perot finished third, but the 19 percent of the popular vote he received was one of the strongest showings by a third-party candidate in American history.

very wealthy individuals. So candidates must find ways to reach out to more and more individuals. The first real push to use the Internet for fund-raising was made by Howard Dean during the 2004 presidential primary race. Dean is widely known as the candidate who proved that Internet fund-raising could be successful. Candidates can raise large sums of money online in a short amount of time with very few expenses.

ADVERTISING AND THE MEDIA

Raising money is considered a crucial element of a successful political campaign. However, statistics indicate that the candidate with the most money doesn't always win. Billionaires Ross Perot and Steve Forbes had unlimited personal funds to spend when they ran for president, but neither was elected. One campaign activity that does require heavy spending is commercial advertising, particularly on television and radio. During the primary races, multiple candidates are competing for name recognition, and advertising can help voters to draw some distinctions between the candidates. Research shows a direct relationship between the amount of money spent for campaign advertising and candidate support among voters.

There are two basic types of candidate advertising—dynamic and static. Dynamic ads show the candidate in multiple scenes with fast cuts from one location or activity to another, usually with music and a narrative voice-over. These often show the candidate interacting with members of the public or depict the candidate as a "regular" person, engaging in some kind of hobby or personal activity with family members. Static ads, by contrast, show the candidate in a single scene, usually sitting or standing still, talking directly into the camera. These ads typically have the candidate discussing policy views or even comparing himself or herself to the opposing candidate.

Research shows that dynamic ads elicit a more positive response from voters than static ads. But that positive response is an emotional reaction only. Static ads require a thoughtful reaction, necessary to understand and evaluate the candidate's position. Campaigns tend to use dynamic ads more often than static ads, with the intention of generating an emotional reaction and forging a connection to the voters.

Most so-called "issue ads" are developed and financed by the political parties and political action committees, rather than the individual candidates. Studies show that the two parties tend to stress the issues that are historically associated with the strengths of the party. Democrats are often thought to do a better job of dealing with issues such as education, poverty, and the environment, while Republicans tend to have the advantage on foreign affairs and national security. Issue ads generally compare and contrast the candidates, showing one candidate more skilled or better suited to address a certain issue. They may often highlight an incumbent's past failures as well. Issue ads may not directly ask the viewer to cast a vote for a particular candidate, but, because of the requirements of the Bipartisan Campaign Reform Act of 2002 (also known as the McCain-Feingold Act), there must be a direct statement in the ad identifying the sponsor. This helps viewers know exactly which group financed the ad, so they can identify the ad's underlying motive and direction.

NEGATIVE ADVERTISING

Negativity has become a routine part of general election campaigns. Unfortunately, the media often pays more attention to the negative

During the 2004 election cycle, Republican George W. Bush ran an attack ad that featured footage of his opponent, John Kerry, windsurfing while on vacation. The ad's narration criticized Kerry for changing his positions on a number of important policy issues, ending with the statement, "John Kerry: Whichever way the wind blows." The Bush campaign effectively painted Kerry as an unprincipled politician, and ended up winning a majority of the popular vote and a 286-251 victory in the Electoral College.

comments that candidates make about each other than they do to the policy statements that candidates make. Personal attacks and conflict make great television. Viewers tend to have an immediate emotional reaction to negativity, rather than the thoughtful reaction needed to understand policy and issue statements.

Despite the common use of negative advertising, research results are mixed regarding its effect on voting preferences. Some studies indicate that negative ads generate voter support, but other studies show just the opposite. Studies also indicate that people remember negative ads better than positive ads. Negative ads that attack a candidate's character are often targeted to run early in the election season. Attacking the opposing candidate early can undermine the voters' trust in that candidate. If the voters don't trust a candidate, it often doesn't matter what stand that candidate takes on a policy issue.

However, research also shows that negative personal attacks can backfire and prompt the voters to distrust the candidate who is behind such attacks. If a candidate relies too heavily on attacking an opponent's character or personality, and seldom discusses policy or issues, voters may wonder whether the attacking candidate is well informed and capable of leading the country.

Negative ads tend to be more effective with voters when they are sponsored by a third party or a source that is not formally part of the candidate's campaign, such as labor unions, nonprofits associated with particular interests, and the national party committee. This distances the candidate from the negativity, making it seem less personal. In addition, negative ads that criticize the policy positions of an opposing candidate are usually more effective than those that criticize the opponent's character or image.

COVERAGE IN THE PRESS

It is also important for candidates to get their names into newspaper stories and television news reports whenever possible. Members of the news media travel with presidential candidates during their journeys across the country as they visit the so-called "battleground states." These are states that could vote either Democratic or Republican, and winning them could swing the election to one side or the other. Reporters for both local and national publications and outlets follow the candidates while they are making speeches and attending public events.

An incumbent often has an advantage over challengers when it comes to attracting free press coverage. The incumbent president receives media coverage almost daily because of the policy decisions, speeches, public appearances and press conferences that are a routine part of daily life in the White House.

Some candidates can generate interest by criticizing their rivals. Attacks and controversy play well on television. When candidates of the same political party are campaigning, they often have similar views on policy and issues. By launching personal attacks against other candidates, they distinguish themselves from their opponents and garner attention from the media.

In addition to following the candidates themselves, the media also reports on the results of opinion polls. Polling is done by the political parties, special-interest groups, the candidates' campaign staff, and media outlets. Polls are used to track candidate support and to highlight important policy issues.

Members of the news media seek quotes from a Republican candidate after a 2015 debate. Statistics show that most voters get a substantial proportion of their news and information from local newspapers, radio, and television stations. Candidates attempt to take advantage of the free publicity that the news media provides by making public appearances, speaking at party fund-raising dinners, attending sporting events, and appearing on local radio and television talk shows.

SPIN AND BIAS

Even though it is less expensive, press coverage is different from paid advertising because the candidate can't control the message. Media executives determine which candidates are featured on their stations or in their publications, thereby controlling who gets the most coverage. These decisions can be influenced by executives' personal preferences and party affiliations. Certain TV stations, radio stations, and newspapers tend to be more liberal; others are more conservative. They put what is called a spin, or slant, on the news. Two different media outlets may report on the same event, but present the facts with entirely different comments. These comments can cast a candidate and his or her actions in a good light or bad light, depending on whether that outlet supports the candidate or not.

Journalists may also respond on a subconscious level, according to their own beliefs and preferences, when reporting on candidates' skills and capabilities. They may get caught up in personality conflicts with individual candidates, since some candidates are better at dealing with the press than others. Another problem with journalists involves their position as interpreters of what the candidates say. Research on recent campaigns shows that for every minute that a candidate speaks, journalists covering the election tend to talk for six minutes on newscasts and shows that feature political commentary. This means the public is often hearing journalists interpret what they think the candidate means, rather than hearing the candidate speak directly and then making their own judgments. Political analysts are almost never neutral. They typically have a strong allegiance to one of the two major political parties, and their comments are skewed by that allegiance.

PUBLICITY THROUGH THE INTERNET

The Internet is an ever-increasing presence in political coverage. Major print and television outlets have a web presence as well. The *New York Times*, the *Washington Post*, and *USA Today* websites are among the most popular for those seeking political information. Websites compete for readers just as other forms of media do. But websites compete in different ways—usually in the race to see who can report news first. This drive to be first can lead to factual errors or conclusions drawn from too little research. Readers must be careful not to form opinions until all the facts are available.

Many websites that are not related to mainstream media outlets can be even less objective. Sites may be run by interest groups, political analysts, law professors, and authors, all writing blogs that are more opinion than news. Rather than taking facts directly from blogs, readers can use those blogs as a source of information about stories available elsewhere on the web that they may have missed. Readers can move from the blogs to other sites to continue checking facts.

Unlike most newspaper journalists, who are supposed to present facts without bias, political commentators such as Rachel Maddow, Sean Hannity, and Ann Coulter generally allow their own ideological beliefs to color their interviews and reports.

Blogging, websites, and email are all important tools also used directly by the candidates. Most candidates now have a blog writer on staff to keep information flowing constantly. Despite the candidates' attempts to use the Internet as a way to reach previously uninterested demographics, research has shown that the Internet has not been effective in luring politically apathetic people into political participation. It doesn't seem to increase voter participation or affect voter decision-making. There is an opportunity for information sharing through chat rooms and other interactive technology, but candidates have been slow to take advantage of this because they cannot control what citizens would add to their sites.

DEBATING THE ISSUES

The news media are also heavily involved in the party debates. The two major parties—the Democrats and the Republicans—each hold a series of debates before the primaries and caucuses. The parties decide how many debates will occur, when they will occur, and who will sponsor them. Typically, news outlets are invited by the parties to be

Candidates for the Republican Party's presidential nomination pose for a photo before a party-sponsored debate in September 2015. There were so many candidates for the party's nomination in 2016 that they could not all be on one stage at the same time.

debate sponsors. The sponsors are allowed to decide which candidates are invited to participate.

Being included in a debate gives a candidate an aura of credibility and a great deal of free media coverage. Sponsors often use opinion poll results to determine who is invited to the debates, particularly if there are a large number of candidates. Inviting only the candidates with the highest poll rankings helps keep the debate manageable.

The debates are an important way for voters to decide between different candidates from the same party. The way the candidates answer questions about policy issues helps point out differences that may not be apparent in paid advertising. Voters can also see candidates interact with each other and determine which ones appear more "presidential."

THE PARTY CONVENTION

The final step in the nomination process for the two major parties is the national convention. The parties hold their conventions after all primaries and caucuses are complete, usually in late summer of the election year. The conventions are held separately several weeks apart in major cities. Party conventions developed as a way for party delegates to agree on a single candidate and on the party's platform. The platform is an official statement of the party's positions on the policies determined to be most important. Each party has a specific formula that determines how many delegates attend the convention from each state, usually based on state population. The delegates arrive at the convention pledged to vote for a specific candidate as determined by the state primaries and caucuses.

In addition to the pledged delegates, each party has delegates that are not pledged to any particular candidate. In the Republican Party, these are called "unpledged delegates." In the Democratic Party, these are called "super delegates." These delegates can vote for whoever

Party conventions generate excitement, build support for the nominated candidate, and publicize the party's platform heading into the general election.

President Gerald Ford and Ronald Reagan shake hands at the end of the Republican National Convention in Kansas City, August 1976. Reagan, the former governor of California, mounted a strong challenge to Ford, the incumbent president, at the convention. Ford would go on to narrowly lose the general election to Democratic Party candidate Jimmy Carter. Four years later, Reagan would gain the Republican nomination and defeat Carter in the 1980 general election to win the presidency.

they like at the convention. They do not have to disclose their choice in advance. Usually these delegates are party leaders or former party candidates from past elections. Some voters don't like the idea of unpledged delegates because they feel these delegates are making a personal decision about who to vote for at the convention and are not required to carry out the wishes of the majority of the party members.

In the past, conventions offered high drama. The primary and caucus systems were different and delegates arrived at the conventions not knowing how the vote would turn out. However, because of the way primaries and caucuses are managed today, there isn't much drama left. The last time a major party's presidential nomination was truly uncertain was at the Republican Party convention of 1976, when Ronald Reagan seriously challenged Gerald Ford, the incumbent president. Although Ford had won more delegates in the primaries, he did not have enough to win the nomination outright. At the start of the convention, both candidates tried to convince unpledged delegates to vote for them. Ford ultimately prevailed, winning the party's nomination with 52 percent of the delegates' votes.

Today, delegates, the media, and the general public know the party nominee way in advance of the convention. The conventions are held primarily to generate enthusiasm for the party, build support for the party's selected candidate, and publicize the party's platform positions. The nomination process often creates rifts within the party, especially if the primaries and caucuses have been bitterly fought between popular candidates. The convention is a time for party members to heal those wounds and rally behind the nominee. The emphasis switches from campaigning and debating among themselves to focusing their efforts on defeating the opposing party's candidate.

The conventions are nationally televised. There are many speeches from party leaders, senators, members of Congress, and governors. The highlight is the roll call vote of each state and the official nomination of the candidate. The candidate then makes an acceptance speech. This speech is usually the beginning of the fight against the opposing party. After the conventions, the parties and their candidates make the final push to the general election.

Chapter 5

The General Election

Once the party conventions are finished in mid-August, that leaves just about twelve weeks until Election Day in November. During this time, both of the candidates will run vigorous campaigns, often visiting numerous places each day and delivering speeches to as many voters as they can. The candidates, the political parties that they represent, and various PACs and organizations that support them will run many advertisements extolling their virtues and attacking their opponent.

If one of the candidates is an incumbent president—as Barack Obama was in 2012 or George W. Bush was in 2004—he has many advantages over a challenger. First, the incumbent rarely has to spend resources and energy winning the party's nomination. This leaves the incumbent with more funds that can be spent later in the campaign season. Another advantage is that the incumbent president is already known by millions of Americans. Some voters don't spend much time researching candidates or following the news. When they vote, they look only for names they recognize.

If the president had a successful first term, and has earned a high approval rating among the citizens, those factors give the incumbent a clear advantage in the general election. The incumbent president can point to the accomplishments of his first term as tangible evidence that he is capable of doing the job as president. The challenger is at a disadvantage, as he or she has never had the opportunity to do this job. Of course, if the incumbent president has not had a successful term or has become entangled in controversy, these factors can be a disadvantage. The incumbent's mistakes give the challenger plenty of ammunition to attack the incumbent's record, and can be used to remind voters about the president's failings.

In recent years some people have expressed concern about the amount of time a current president must spend campaigning for a second term instead of governing. It is estimated that as much as one-fourth of the current term must be used to campaign for the next one; that is basically one year out of four. Three major outreach offices are included in the White House staff: the Office of Communications, the Office of Public Liaison, and the Office of Political Affairs. The staff of these offices advise the current president on both governing and managing the campaign. During the campaign, the president and the White House staff must be constantly aware that there is no separation between campaign politics and governing. Any decisions made on policy will immediately become part of the campaign, providing a boost in approval for the president or giving competitors fuel for their attacks. The president is also subject to being second-guessed by analysts who may attempt to claim that executive decisions are made based on what is best for the campaign, rather than what is best for the country and its citizens.

THE GENERAL ELECTION DEBATES

Just as during the primary season, the two major party candidates participate in a series of debates on policy issues. These debates are televised, and are viewed by millions of Americans. The presidential debates are usually held during October. Traditionally, there are three separate debates involving the presidential candidates: one that focuses on domestic issues, another that focuses on foreign affairs, and a third that allows questions on all topics. Usually, a debate between the vice presidential candidates is held around the same time.

Republican presidential candidate Mitt Romney arrives at a campaign event in Dayton, Ohio, during September 2012. The candidates spend the months after the party convention in a flurry of activity, visiting as many states as they can in order to win over undecided voters.

Since 1987, the presidential debates between the nominated candidates have been sponsored and produced by the Commission on Presidential Debates (CPD). The CPD is a private, nonprofit organization. It is not funded by any political action committee, political party, or candidate. The money to operate CPD is donated by private citizens and corporations. The CPD also collects fees from the locations selected to host the debates.

Debates are not required by the Constitution. Prior to 1987, the candidates from the two major parties negotiated among themselves about the timing and format of the debates. When the parties were unable to reach an agreement, there were no debates at all. In 1987, the leaders of the Democratic and Republican National Committees

John McCain and Barack Obama participate in one of the 2008 presidential debates.

agreed to transfer control of the debates to an independent commission and the CPD was formed.

The number of debates and the locations are determined separately for each presidential election. The CPD reviews the success of the previous debates and determines when changes need to be made to the format or schedule. Bids to host the debates are requested from specific locations, usually colleges and universities. The Board of Directors reviews the bids and determines how many debates will be held and picks the final locations.

Not all candidates are invited to participate in the debates. The CPD sets the selection criteria, determining which candidates participate in the debates. These criteria change slightly with each election. But a few basic criteria remain the same: (1) The candidate must meet the presidential eligibility requirements set by the Constitution, (2) the candidate must appear on the ballots of enough states to make sure that they have a chance to win, and (3) the candidate must rank high enough in an average of several of the national opinion polls to be considered a "serious" candidate by the voters. Typically, the CPD averages the percentages of support from five national polls and invites only candidates who have the support of at least 15 percent of the voters.

Presidential candidates are not required to participate. However, the debates are nationally televised and the exposure on national television is an important, and free, resource for the candidates. Many political analysts consider the candidates' performance in the debates as a critical factor in gaining or losing votes.

Invited candidates almost always agree to participate. In fact, the only person who has ever refused to participate in a presidential debate was incumbent President Jimmy Carter in 1980. Carter was unhappy that the debate would also include third-party candidate John Anderson, so the first debate of 1980 was between Anderson and Republican candidate Ronald Reagan, with an empty chair on stage signifying the missing president. Carter did agree to participate in a debate with Reagan in late October because Anderson was excluded from this event.

The CPD selects a person to serve as moderator for the event. The moderator controls the flow of the debate, keeping candidate responses under control and making sure each candidate follows the rules established by the news organization sponsoring the debate. The moderator is usually someone with a lot of experience in television broadcast news, oftentimes a major network news anchor. The moderator formulates the questions that will be asked of the candidates, together with the other members of the panel of journalists. Immediately following the debates, the major news networks host forums analyzing the candidates' performances.

VOTING ON ELECTION DAY

Every four years, U.S. citizens go to their local polling places to cast their ballots and select their preferred candidate for president. Although voting for their leaders is considered one of the most important acts a citizen can do, the rate of participation in American elections has declined significantly over the past fifty years. In the past few presidential elections, only about 58 percent of the Americans who are eligible to vote actually cast ballots. In the mid-year elections for Congress and other federal offices, the rate of voter participation is even lower.

Signs point the way for people who want to take advantage of early voting. In the 2016 presidential election, early voting will be available in thirty-three states plus the District of Columbia. Supporters of early voting say it reduces the lengths of lines on election day and makes the process less stressful for both voters and poll workers. They believe it can increase voter turnout.

In 1845 Congress passed a law that established Election Day as the Tuesday following the first Monday in November. Tuesday was selected because during the nineteenth century America was a farming nation, and many people did not live in cities or towns. Citizens who had registered to vote had to travel from rural areas to a designated place, known as a precinct, to physically cast their ballots. Sunday was set aside for religious services, and Wednesday was usually market day, so Tuesday was chosen as the most convenient day. The fall harvest was completed in late October, and the winter snows had not yet started, so November was a month that would not interfere with farming practices and would be an easy month for travel.

Voting practices in the United States remained mostly the same from the mid-nineteenth century until about twenty years ago. At that time, it had become clear that many citizens were not voting because they could not get away from work or because there was bad weather that day, or because the lines were too long, or any one of a number of other reasons. Election officials decided that voter turnout would improve if voting became more convenient. Today, in most states voters who are going to be away from home on Election Day can mail in absentee ballots ahead of the election. In some states, people are permitted to cast their votes during the weeks before Election Day at special early-voting locations. Disabled voters can register to vote by phone in some states. These tactics are known as convenience voting, and in 2012 they were used by more than 30 percent of all registered voters.

Even with the greater availability of convenience voting, some voting activists believe voter turnout is still affected by the Tuesday vote, especially among lower-income citizens. A bill was introduced in Congress in 2005 to make Election Day a national holiday, called Democracy Day. This would at least solve the problem for most voters of having to take off from work. However, the proposed law never made it to a final vote and was abandoned. It has also been suggested that the existing law should be changed to move Election Day to Saturday. However, no changes have yet been made.

After casting their own ballots, volunteers for the candidates will spend Election Day making phone calls to registered voters, encouraging them to go to the polls and vote. Voter turnout is an important part of a winning campaign strategy.

The individual states set the hours that the polling places are open. Often, during presidential elections the polling places are open early in the morning, so that people can vote before they go to work. The polls often don't close until 8 or 9 o'clock at night, so that people have time to vote after work. The poll hours may be shorter in mid-term elections, or in separate elections for state or local officials.

AFTER THE VOTES HAVE BEEN CAST

For those who are interested in politics, Election Night is always very exciting. The major news outlets have live coverage of the election, reporting on the progress of the vote as the polls close in each state. Each outlet wants to be the first to report the results from the battle-ground states.

Even before the polls officially close, reporters try to predict which candidate will win each state. The concept of "exit polling" was developed during the 1960s as a way to identify early results. Voters were asked to complete cards as they left the polling places to tell pollsters which candidate they had selected. This was considered an effective system to predict the winner before the official vote counts were completed.

The major news outlets joined together to create the News Election Service in 1964. This group, under the direction of polling specialists, was responsible for conducting the exit polls and reporting the results back to the networks. An improved and expanded service called the Voter News Service was established in 1993. This system appeared to work relatively well until the controversial presidential election of 2000. Because of the very close vote in the key battle-ground state of Florida, the lead changed several times. The different media outlets were each trying to beat one another in announcing the winner, and several mistakes were made. The Voter News Service was closed and the outlets established a new group of polling specialists to operate the new National Election Poll (NEP) in 2003.

By the time the NEP initiated its improved exit polling methods, the idea of exit polls had fallen out of favor. A panel of former politicians and elections experts that was formed after the 2000 election,

Exit polling and post-vote interviews have fallen out of favor in recent years. In the 2000 election, the media rushed to declare a winner in some states before the voting had even ended. Their reports may have led some people who had not yet voted to stay home, believing that their vote would not make a difference in the outcome.

called the National Commission on Federal Election Reforms, even called for citizens to refuse to participate in exit polling. The Commission was concerned about the early identification of the winning candidate based on results in the Eastern time zone, where the polls typically close three hours earlier than polls in the Pacific time zone. Analysts claimed that exit polling and predictions could directly affect an election if voters on the West Coast decided not to vote because they believed the election had already been decided.

The growing trend of convenience voting makes exit polls even less reliable. The results of early voting, absentee voting, and telephone voting are not available at the time exit polls are taken. Exit poll information is taken only from voters leaving the designated precinct location on Election Day itself. To make the information more accurate, most analysts believe it would be necessary to supplement exit polls with telephone polling to try to get numbers associated with convenience voting. But this is very expensive and difficult to implement. It has also been shown that only about one in ten people contacted will actually respond to a telephone survey.

Exit polling has not been completely abandoned. In the wake of the National Commission on Federal Election Reforms study, news outlets have agreed to be less aggressive about identifying the winner

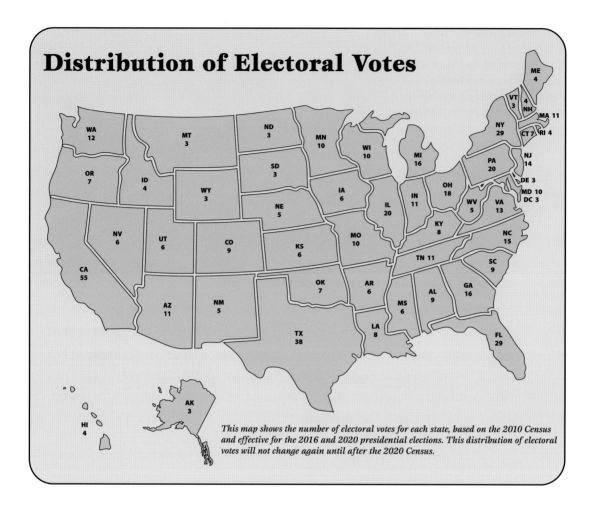

Distribution of Electoral Votes

This map shows the number of electoral votes for each state, based on the 2010 Census and effective for the 2016 and 2020 presidential elections. This distribution of electoral votes will not change again until after the 2020 Census.

early. Most have agreed to delay projecting a winner in any state until all the polls have closed in that state. Election reform activists have challenged the news outlets to stop identifying an overall winner until the polls have closed in all states, hoping to avoid some problems from the past. As the 2016 presidential election approaches, the NEP is researching more accurate ways to identify voting statistics, including the use of Internet polling.

THE ELECTORAL COLLEGE VOTE

After the popular vote is completed in a state, the votes are counted. In most cases, the candidate who wins the most votes in a state receives all of that state's electoral votes. Two states, Maine and Nebraska, may split their electoral votes. These states each allocate two electoral votes to the candidate that wins the popular vote statewide. They also allocate one electoral vote to the popular vote winner in each of the state's Congressional districts. (Maine has two Congressional districts, while Nebraska has three.) Maine has never split its Electoral votes, but in 2008 Barack Obama won one of Nebraska's Congressional districts, so he received one of the state's electoral votes while John McCain—who won 56 percent of the vote statewide—received four electoral votes.

The president is formally chosen by the Electoral College, a group of electors picked by the political parties in each state. These are usually people who are active in the party. The Electoral College vote is specifically required by the Constitution. Each state is allowed a certain number of electoral votes. That number is based on the state's population, which also determines its representation in Congress. The higher the state's population, the more representatives it has in Congress and the higher number of electoral votes it receives.

The population of each state is based on the most recent national census, which is conducted every ten years. For example, based on its population in the 2010 census, Virginia has eleven members in the House of Representatives, plus two members in the Senate (as all states have). Therefore, Virginia is allotted thirteen electors, who each have a vote in the Electoral College. Each state, no matter how small its population, is allotted at least three electoral votes.

In mid-December, electors from all over the country meet in Washington, D.C., to officially cast their ballots. The electors are bound by tradition to vote only for the candidate who won the popular vote in their state. However, sometimes an elector will vote for another candidate instead of the one that he or she had promised to support. This is known as a "faithless elector." In 1976, for example, an elector from Washington who was pledged to vote for the Republican candidate Gerald Ford cast his vote for Ronald Reagan (who had challenged Ford during the Republican primary) instead. The phenomenon of the faithless elector is fairly rare, and has never affected the outcome of a presidential election.

There are a total of 538 electoral votes. A candidate must collect at least 270 electoral votes to become president. If no candidate receives at least 270 electoral votes, the members of the House of Representatives must vote to determine the winner. In that case, each state gets a single vote. That vote does not have to be cast for the winner of the popular vote in that state. House members from each state can make their own decision as to who to vote for.

CHANGING THE ELECTORAL COLLEGE SYSTEM

The Electoral College system was written into the U.S. Constitution by the founding fathers. The system was developed to make sure that candidates took a moderate stand on policy issues. The founding fathers believed that the Electoral College system would force candidates to avoid backing narrow interests of just one part of the country or just one ethnic group or just one economic group. However, the country has changed considerably in the last 200 years. Some people feel the country has outgrown the need for the Electoral College.

There is widespread support for abandoning the Electoral College and deciding the election directly by the popular vote. One major criticism is that only about sixteen states account for the majority of electoral votes. California, New York, Texas, and Florida have large numbers of electoral votes, followed by Pennsylvania, Illinois, Ohio, Michigan, Georgia, North Carolina, New Jersey, Virginia, Washington, Arizona, Massachusetts, and Tennessee. In addition to these sixteen states, Iowa and New Hampshire are considered battleground states because of the early dates of their caucus and primary, respectively. Candidates typically campaign heavily in these states, addressing issues important to those voters and ignoring other states and issues. This keeps the election from being about the entire country and instead forces the candidates to focus their attention on a relatively small number of states.

However, changing the Electoral College system is difficult. Eliminating the Electoral College would require a constitutional amendment, and amendments are very difficult to pass. A constitutional amendment may be proposed by a two-thirds majority vote in both the House of Representatives and the Senate, called a "joint resolution." It may also be proposed at a constitutional convention, called for by two-thirds of the states and convened by Congress. So far there have been twenty-seven amendments to the Constitution, all proposed by congressional joint resolutions.

The president does not have a role in determining whether a constitutional amendment will be proposed or approved. The joint resolution proposing an amendment does not go to the White House for approval. The document goes directly to the Office of the Federal Register for printing under the direction of the National Archives. An information packet is also prepared, explaining the background for the amendment. The archivist sends the proposed amendment and the information packet to the state governors. The governors then formally submit the proposal to the state legislatures. The amendment must be approved (a process called ratification) by three-fourths of the states (thirty-eight out of fifty). The states return their approvals to the archivist and a certification is prepared for the president's signature. There have been 700 proposals presented in Congress to amend the Constitution to change the Electoral College system. None of these proposals have received enough votes to even move to the joint resolution stage.

THE PROPOSED NATIONAL POPULAR VOTE

A special-interest group called the National Popular Vote is trying to bring about change through a different strategy. Statistics gathered by the group showed that in the 2004 presidential election, the candidates spent 99 percent of their money and 92 percent of their time in the sixteen battleground states. During the 2012 campaign, the statistics showed that out of a total of 253 campaign events, 176 were held in just the four states of Ohio, Florida, Virginia, and Iowa. In 38 states, no events were held at all. These statistics show the candidates virtually ignored the voters outside the battleground states. The proponents of the National Popular Vote claim a different system would force candidates to campaign seriously in every state, making the election more inclusive.

National Popular Vote Agreements

Legend:
- Signed National Vote Agreement
- National Vote Agreement pending in legislature

Data as of January 2016. Source: www.nationalpopularvote.com

Rather than backing a constitutional amendment to do away with the Electoral College, the group sponsoring the National Popular Vote has devised a way for the Electoral College vote to match the national popular vote. The plan was proposed in 2006 and supported by a group including former senators and representatives, a former independent presidential candidate, and members of Common Cause and the League of Women Voters. The plan was to gather support for an agreement among states to pledge their electoral votes to the winner of the national popular vote. Each state's electors would be bound to the winner of the national vote. The state would pledge its votes in the Electoral College to the candidate who won the overall national popular vote, not necessarily the winner of the popular vote in that state.

That way, the winner of the popular vote would be the winner of the electoral vote and would be elected president.

The National Popular Vote plan does not go against the Constitution because the Constitution specifically gives states control over how their electoral votes are awarded. At the time the plan was first proposed, forty-eight states had state laws requiring all their electoral votes to be awarded to the winner of the popular vote in their state. Maine and Nebraska had laws awarding their electoral votes to the candidate winning the popular vote in each district. Under these statutes, the national vote totals do not figure into the awarding of electoral votes. The National Popular Vote agreement would change that.

The National Popular Vote proposal does not require a constitutional amendment and therefore no congressional action. But the plan does have to be passed by each state's legislature to override the existing state laws. Opinion polls indicate that the agreement has widespread support, with over 70 percent of the nation's registered voters in favor of the change. As of September 2015, eleven states had National Popular Vote agreements passed by their state legislatures and signed by their governors.

These eleven states represent 105 electoral votes, or 61 percent of the 270 votes needed for a majority. It is interesting to note that this list includes states with high, medium, and low numbers of allotted electoral votes. This indicates widespread support for this proposal among the state legislators across the country, regardless of a state's population.

Several more states have National Popular Vote proposals pending in their state legislatures, but it is unlikely that these will be passed and signed prior to the 2016 presidential election. In order for the proposal to take effect, states totalling at least 270 electoral votes—the amount needed for an electoral majority—must have signed laws in place. Until that mark is reached, the agreement is not valid and all states must continue adhering to the current arrangement. It is doubtful that the required number will be reached by November 2016. Progress toward approval of the National Popular Vote agreement may be followed at www.NationalPopularVote.com.

Chapter 6

Inauguration

The Twentieth Amendment to the U.S. Constitution sets the starting date of the president's term as January 20. The amendment was passed in 1933 and took effect in 1937. The first day of the president's service is called Inauguration Day. Inauguration Day is marked by a specific set of public and private events, the most important being the swearing-in ceremony, during which the president-elect takes the oath of office. If January 20 falls on a Sunday, there is usually a private ceremony for the taking of the oath, with the public events celebrated on Monday.

The inauguration celebration is planned and executed by the Joint Congressional Committee on Inaugural Ceremonies. Each inauguration has a slightly different theme and tone, depending on what is hap-

The public ceremonies of the presidential inauguration are always held on January 20, unless that date falls on a Sunday. (Top) With his family by his side, President George W. Bush is sworn in for his second term as the 43rd President of the United States by U.S. Supreme Court Chief Justice William Rehnquist, 2005. (Bottom) Barack and Michelle Obama walk in the inaugural parade on Pennsylvania Avenue that follows the swearing-in ceremony, 2013.

Every four years, large crowds of Americans visit Washington, D.C., to observe the presidential inauguration ceremony on January 20.

pening in the country and the world at the time. But over the past fifty years, a standard set of events have become traditional. The day typically starts with the president-elect and his or her family attending an early-morning religious service of their choice. Following the service, the president-elect, the vice president–elect, and their spouses meet briefly with the outgoing president at the White House. Then the group travels to the U.S. Capitol for the swearing-in ceremony.

The new vice president is sworn in first, usually by a friend or a political associate. Then the new president is sworn in by the chief justice of the Supreme Court. The ceremony takes place outside, on the steps of the Capitol, on a specially constructed platform. The president takes the oath with his or her hand on a Bible. The wording of the oath of office is specifically mandated by Article II, Section 1 of the Constitution. The chief justice leads the president-elect through the wording of the oath: "I do solemnly swear [or affirm] that I will faithfully execute the office of president of the United States, and will to the best of my ability, preserve, protect, and defend the Constitution of the United States."

Following the oath, the new president gives an Inaugural Address, a speech setting out his vision and goals for the upcoming presidential term. Following the address, the president and vice president escort the former president out of the Capitol, then return for a private lunch, hosted by the inaugural committee. After lunch, the president and vice president take part in a parade from the Capitol grounds back to the White House. That evening the president, the vice president, and their families and invited guests attend several parties.

CONCLUSION

Inauguration Day marks the official end of the election and the beginning of the new president's term in office. It is the culmination of almost two years of work by the candidates and their staff, the political party committees, the media, interest groups, and the voters. The campaign has been waged, the voters have made their choice, and the American election process has completed a change in the highest governing office in the country without violence or social unrest. There is no other country in the world with the same process. The change in governing power in many other counties is violent and disruptive, not only to government but also to the daily lives of citizens.

The presidential election process isn't perfect. Changes will always be needed, proposed, and debated. Some will be implemented, but the goal of the process will remain the same: an orderly, peaceful change based on the choices of the voters. According to our third president, Thomas Jefferson,

> . . . laws and institutions must go hand in hand with the progress of the human mind. As that becomes more developed, more enlightened, as new discoveries are made, new truths discovered and manners and opinions change with the change of circumstances, institutions must advance also to keep pace with the times.

Thomas Jefferson was one of our founding fathers, and his ideas influenced the writing of the Constitution and the development of our system of government. But Jefferson recognized the need for the system to change over time, and to be flexible enough to respond to the needs of American citizens. Those citizens must be directly involved if that change is to be responsive and effective. And to be fully involved, citizens must be informed.

Chronology

1787 The U.S. Constitution is adopted on September 17.

1790 The Naturalization Act of 1790 clarifies that children born to U.S. citizens while traveling or living outside the United States are considered "natural born citizens."

1804 The Twelfth Amendment to the U.S. Constitution modifies the procedure for electing the president and vice president of the United States.

1845 Congress passes the law establishing the first Tuesday following the first Monday in November as presidential Election Day.

1868 The Fourteenth Amendment to the Constitution grants citizenship to people "naturalized" in the United States. The naturalization process involves completion of an application and a written test, following a mandatory residency period in the United States.

1898 The Supreme Court ruling in *United States v. Wong Kim Ark* establishes that children born in the United States to non-U.S. citizens are automatically considered natural-born citizens.

1937 The Twentieth Amendment to the Constitution sets January 20 as the president's first day in office (Inauguration Day). Previously, presidential inaugurations had been held on March 4, the date on which the Constitution took effect in 1789.

1951 The Twenty-Second Amendment to the Constitution limits the president to two terms in office.

1976 Ronald Reagan seriously challenges the incumbent, Gerald Ford, for the Republican Party's presidential nomination, creating drama at the Republican National Convention. Since then, the conventions have diminished in significance, as the parties' nominees are typically determined months in advance.

1987 The Commission on Presidential Debates (CPD) takes over management of the general election debates from the political parties.

2002 The Bipartisan Campaign Reform Act, also known as the McCain-Feingold Act, sets limits on political party fund-raising and requires that sponsors of political advertisements be specifically identified.

2005 A bill is introduced in Congress to make presidential Election Day a national holiday, called Democracy Day. The bill does not make it to a final vote and is abandoned.

2006 The National Popular Vote agreement is proposed as a way to align the Electoral College vote directly with the results of the popular vote.

2011 The Congressional Research Service publishes a report on its interpretation of the "natural born citizen" presidential eligibility requirement in the U.S. Constitution.

Glossary

ballot—the listing of candidates running for office, used by voters to make their official selection.

battleground states—states in which two major political parties have similar levels of support among voters, so either candidate could win the state's electoral votes.

caucus—a meeting of registered members of a state's political party, in which the candidates are discussed and votes cast to determine a party nominee.

census—an official count of the population of the United States.

closed primary—a secret ballot vote to nominate party candidates in which only registered party members may participate.

convenience voting—a term that refers to alternative methods to voting on Election Day at an official voting precinct location. These include casting absentee ballots by mail, telephone voting, or early voting.

Electoral College—a group of selected delegates who vote, by state, to directly elect the president of the United States as mandated by the Constitution, based on the results of the popular vote by U.S. citizens.

front-loaded primaries—primaries that are held between January and March of a presidential election year.

inauguration—the day in which a newly elected president takes the oath of office, often marked by ceremonies, parades, and parties.

incumbent—someone who holds a political office and is campaigning for reelection.

naturalized citizen—a foreign-born citizen of another country who has become a citizen of the United States by living a minimum numbers of years in the United States and completing a legal application process and citizenship test.

open primary—a secret ballot vote to nominate party candidates in which voters are not required to declare their party affiliation.

party convention—a meeting of the members of a political party for the purpose of nominating the presidential candidate, voting on the party's platform, and generating excitement and support for the general election.

platform—an official statement of a political party's positions on important issues.

political action committee (PAC)—An organization created by corporations, labor unions, or special-interest groups specifically to raise funds for political candidates.

semi-closed primary—a secret ballot vote to nominate party candidates in which both registered party members and independents may participate.

semi-open primary—a secret ballot vote to nominate party candidates in which any registered voter may participate, but in which each voter must request a specific party ballot during check-in at the voting location.

super delegates—delegates to a party convention that are not required to vote for a particular candidate, unlike delegates who are pledged to vote for a candidate chosen in their state's primary or caucus. Also called "unpledged delegates."

Super Tuesday—nickname for the first Tuesday in March of the presidential election year. As many as fifteen states hold their primaries or caucuses on this date.

Further Reading

Bardes, Barbara, Mack Shelly, and Steffen Schmidt. *American Government and Politics Today: Essentials 2015-16 Edition.* Boston: Cengage Learning, 2015.

Erikson, Robert S., and Christopher Wlezien. *The Timeline of Presidential Elections: How Campaigns Do (and Do Not) Matter.* Chicago: University of Chicago Press, 2012.

Genovese, Michael A., and Lori Cox Han. *Encyclopedia of American Government and Civics.* New York: Facts on File, 2008.

La Raja, Raymond J. *Small Change: Money, Political Parties, and Campaign Finance Reform.* Ann Arbor: University of Michigan Press, 2008.

Polsby, Nelson W., et al. *Presidential Elections: Strategies and Structures of American Politics.* Lanham, Md.: Rowman and Littlefield, 2015.

Schulman, Marc. *A History of American Presidential Elections: From George Washington to Barack Obama.* New Rochelle, NY: MultiEducator, 2013.

Internet Resources

http://www.fec.gov

    The Federal Election Commission (FEC) is an independent regulatory agency created to enforce the provisions of campaign laws and oversee the funding of presidential elections.

https://www.democrats.org

    Home page of the Democratic National Committee (DNC), an organization that provides leadership for the Democratic Party. The DNC coordinates national fundraising efforts and election strategy. It also develops and promotes the party platform, a list of its positions on various current issues.

https://www.gop.com

    The home page of the Republican National Committee, which provides leadership for the party. It includes articles about Republican candidates, as well as the Republican position on current issues, known as the party platform.

http://www.electoral-vote.com

    This site tracks political polls for U.S. federal elections. Both national and state polls are followed, with a regularly updated color-coded map showing how each candidate is faring.

Index

Numbers in **bold italic** refer to captions.

About the Author

Holly Lynn Anderson is a freelance writer living in Arkansas with her two dogs, her garden, and far too many books. Educated in technical and scientific writing, her interests extend to environmental conservation, history, anthropology, and all things paranormal.